Unfamiliar Weather

# Unfamiliar
## WEATHER

CHRIS HUTCHINSON

The Muses' Company Series Editor: Catherine Hunter
Book design by Terry Gallagher/Doowah Design Inc.
Cover image from photograph, Riverside Quay, Hull (C)1975-83, by Peter Marshall, buildingsoflondon.co.uk
Printed and bound in Canada

We acknowledge the financial support of the Manitoba Arts Council, The Canada Council for the Arts and the Government of Canada through the Book Publishing Industry Development Program (BPIDP) for our publishing program.

Library and Archives Canada Cataloguing in Publication

Hutchinson, Chris, 1972-
Unfamiliar weather/Chris Hutchinson.

Poems.
ISBN 0-920486-82-7

I. Title.
PS88615.U82U53 2005 C811'.6 C2005-900543-2

J. Gordon Shillingford Publishing
P.O. Box 86, RPO Corydon Avenue, Winnipeg, MB Canada R3M 3S3

Everyone is so
lonely in this
country that
it's necessary
to be fantastic

— John Newlove

# Acknowledgments

Earlier versions of some of these poems appeared in *The Antigonish Review, Event, The Fiddlehead, Geist, Grain, The New Quarterly, Pottersfield Portfolio,* PRISM *International, Qwerty and subTerrain*; in the chapbooks *Season of Strangers* (Smoking Lung Press, 1998) and *Nowhere But Here* (Mosquito Press, 2004); and in the anthologies *Hammer & Tongs* (Smoking Lung Press, 1999) and *Breathing Fire 2* (Nightwood, 2004).

This book would not have been possible without support from the following people: Brad Cran, Rodney DeCroo, Patrick Friesen, Aislinn Hunter, my editor Catherine Hunter, Eve Joseph, William Knowles, Donato Mancini, Teresa McWhirter, Billeh Nickerson, Marguerite Pigeon, and Matt Rader.

Thanks also to the Banff Centre for the Arts, where several of these poems were drafted.

Most of all I'd like to thank my family for their unflagging belief in whatever it is that I supposedly do.

# Table of Contents

FOUR

~1~

# Small Burdens

## Monday: The Weather

You read with the page turned
upside-down, craving a different perspective.
Your eyes have starved all winter. You grew a garden
of bright obsessions to nourish the fragile sun.
How you staggered delirious to meet the spring.
How early in love you once mastered an excess impossible
to retract. Then, waking up this morning
beneath the unfamiliar weather full of strange birds
knifing their brilliant wings inside your chest,
how you wished only to sleep again.

## Tuesday: Politics

Everything opposes sense.
You live in an airless stupor, get unhinged
when the infirm meek or destitute
become articulate while our leaders squawk
and squelch like radios on the fritz.
Today, bus fare went up again, it's rained
the last ten days of June and your neighbourhood floods
with heroin and cops. So where should you complain?
Is it best to write your Ombudsman or just throw stones
at the Milky Way? Like most,
you have no voice for politics,
just hurts.

## Wednesday: The Bus

On the Main street bus the smells
of fast food, sweat and booze soften the air.
You practice a nullified stare, think,
*Life is grim,* again and again. The bus
jolts to a sudden stop. Some shriek. The driver bellows
like a TV wrestler at someone trying to cross the road:
*Do you want to die? I'll bloody run you down next time!*
People smile and shake their heads. An awkward sense
of knowing pervades, that any day, for anyone,
it could come like this. And the girl
in a nearby seat almost smiles at you then looks
away. You think she could have been
on the cover of some glossy fashion magazine
if it wasn't for the evil scar across her throat—
a necklace of numb flesh you know
she always knows is there, difficult as fact.
Like a small confession she is
truly beautiful inside
the silence you all share.

## Thursday: The Date

You're insane and no one understands.
Does she understand? You explain
you're just like her when you're half-in-love
and bird song nibbles at the morning's edge.
She's not impressed. So maybe she's the one who's mad,
half-way to the moon and never turning back?
You're just like that! Perhaps,
she says, but you have no idea
what it's like to be wholly afraid
and looking down at all you've left behind,
the earth, dropping like your last coin, down
into a bottomless sky.

## Friday: Work

Is this all there is? Squeezing life
into the cracks, into the small openings of the day:
quick revenge, quick amends, a fast try
at humour and nine winks between shifts? *Work*
*is the curse of the drinking class* your father always said, or
was it Oscar Wilde? Regardless, since you quit the booze
you no longer qualify. And love? A surrender to someone
who will more boldly than you deny your faults and despise
your enemies? How such cowardly dreams belie
your righteous independence. At home you read
only poets whose lives have been a mess, who drank
and left their jobs and wives for selfishness. Such love is yours.
Yet every way of life carries a common thread—
every cigarette butt on the street, a remnant of someone
with a role to bear, so that tomorrow, free from work
you'll walk this crowded city, amazed
at everyone you see.

## Saturday: The Movies

Life is tough. The earth is flat. Death is a fantasy.
Everywhere American movie stars kill
with no remorse. They are beautiful and kind.
You hate them without knowing why
the way you hate the parts of yourself
that never change. Your clenched fist,
as ineffectual as the moon, but cigarettes are good,
and rain falls upon the blackened street like
the soundtrack from a sadder world. Who knows
what's real or what's a passing craze? Perhaps everything
will change overnight, our heroes grow benign, their rage
spent. Perhaps beyond America still lie
undiscovered continents.

## Sunday: Art

You read each page last line to first
to see if this makes more sense, feel
your small world spinning apart
around a deep-felt nothingness you consider
art. Each moment is an arrow pointing
in two directions, your name, a word
that wants all language to stop.
Can there be a centre to this series
of careless blunders, these many calamities
you've enacted and re-enacted since birth?
Some days you think you are wise
to live like this, as best you can somewhere
between uncertainty and grace.
Some days are small burdens
of light.

## Residency

That winged skier, the tourist
brochure inside us all, promises
eternal lift, life
          in the unhurried, glacier backdrop
of the sky.
          Listen: under centuries
of freeze, limestone balloons pop up above, boulders
like knuckles cracking before a fight. This could be
          our final warning, our first hint of something
strange afoot clambering up beyond the clouds, or
a day in the life of Banff
in May. Mock-menacingly,
          the magpie skips in fits and spurts, startles
a groundhog into flight—the magpie, jocular
as a *flâneur* wearing a tuxedo
back to front. Meanwhile,
downtown
          residents, elk,
parallel park themselves
between winter and spring, heads held high,
totemic eyes blackly-bulged, a dumb challenge
to passers-by.
                    Why weren't we taught
to scuttle and look away like movie stars
escaping the press? This ecology demands
a new kind of intelligence: namely a droll sense of self-
preservation and spatial
awareness.
          Home? Hotel Insomnia. Take the elevator
or climb the stairs to an arid restlessness
where electricity floats just above the surface
                    of events: phosphorescent
as the ghosts of jellyfish, stingers dipped in blue, in night-
material. Homeless? How the stars
crystallize,
          drift down
from the snowline, tap-tap at our windows,
wanting in.

# A Day in a Life With or Without Love

Start with what's true: a flat white, high
overcast sky and the same dogged loneliness

that follows at the heels of your heart, faithful
as nicotine addiction, a feeling accurate

as a narcissist's mirror. Now, consider
the unlikely: check the want ads, wanting

more, scour the *I Saw You*s, invent
a pseudonym then write a letter to every

famous author you feel guilty about
having never read and ask them

if they've heard of you. Force yourself
out-of-doors, to scissor your arms thru

the prickling air, to observe the soft
geometry of passing faces like pale flames,

to breathe in the as-of-yet unrotting
smell of early autumn's just fallen leaves.

Back home, a lover will visit or she
won't, remembering the last time *you* called.

Remind yourself: this mood is valid but
it is improbable that nothing matters beyond

your sad fidelity. At night, dive in,
swim toward regret. Soon her name

will shiver from the depths like a silver coin
punctuating this cursive script of moonlight

which is the poem your body writes
traipsing like a caress over the water's skin.

## Disclosure

My friend, always the artist, shows me pictures
of his wife—erotic portraits,
he calls them, claims he wants me
to understand the other side
of his married life, the endless
contorting shapes of a desire free
from orthodox modesty. In his eyes
I catch a glint of pride, the roguish
flouting of convention, the smirk
of the saboteur at having infiltrated
the system in order to disrupt it
from within. But there is also a look
of sadness, the underlying grief
of one whose triumphs have come
and gone without praise.
            I inspect each photograph
carefully, affect detachment, knowing
that what I hold between us is clearly more
than what either of us will admit. I see his wife
is beautiful, limbs poised as you would expect
of a woman proffering herself to the idea
of undiluted lasciviousness. Only her smile
betrays the mood, her tentative mouth
which holds the beginning
of a question, like the uncertainty
that occurs after desire but before
contentment begins. With the last
picture in my hands, I pause,
just long enough to see
who will be the first to laugh
or blush. But no one does.

How I love my friend! In his sadness
I recognize the silence common
to us both, the quietly entrenched
resignation, a kind of defeat
I'm sick of not talking about. Because now
I'm craving full disclosure, for the moment
to move beyond taboo. I'm waiting
to see if he'll admit bewilderment
at the day he arrived unprepared
for the end of youth's recklessness
and the beginning of an ache
he couldn't explain, admit
the vulnerability all men conceal
behind displays of experience, our need
for affection carried like a secret shame.
Now I'm waiting for someone to let it all
hang out, to confess aloud. For once,
I'd like to hear it said.

# The Idea of Forever

After last call at three a.m. the sun
on the horizon like a giant lodestar
would guide us over uneven boardwalks and dirt roads
toward the George Black ferry, across
the mud-fed Yukon river to where our hidden world
of tents lay inside a maze of birch,
where branches knocked and clacked in the wind
like the restless bones of ghosts,
where someone always screamed blue-murder
at the land-locked sled dogs as they cried
and howled at the lingering season
and stunning lack of darkness
inside the night. This was Dawson City
where we'd all come from something
vague: a town, a girl, a life.
Most had simply drifted into the ever-
widening space of summer's north, hoping
to find work, hoping absence,
hard drinking and perpetual light could
wipe the slate clean: It seemed we were all young
enough to trust in the liberty of forgetfulness—
the days blurring without nights, drinking
sour-toes with the tourists then
over-proof whiskey at the Midnight Sun then
black-outs and waking beside the river
if not delighted, at least surprised
to be alive, soaked and numb.
Had it been a dream, strange-throated ravens
gargling in the trees like drowning men,
or just some lone person
weeping?
            In the morning,
no one could be sure.
Although I confess, one night
the first star appeared, an unsightly blemish
in the milky sky like a pinprick in the idea
of forever: Fall was coming and I was afraid
to travel south, to move alone again,
and further toward the slowly diminishing
light.

## Static

Anna has a touch of pneumonia
and requests that I come over with
cigarettes. Ground above means sky
below and lungs annealed with liquid
fire. It's Wednesday night again
between television stations, a safe
electric enclave, radiation peaceful
as an oxygen tent or an underwater bubble
of blue light. Our cigarette tips
mark the air, little red stop signs
inside a shifting labyrinth
of highways, spreading pollutants, pathogens,
            parthenogenesis. Our lips kiss
the stale air. We exhale deeply sighs
the size of thoughtless resignation. Anna says
Take the switcher, it's your turn to drive
then turns and rattles the stars inside her chest,
breathes like a chandelier
in an earthquake
that never ends.

# Thirteen Spiders

1.
A spider slowly spun a web
in the corner above the end
of my bed as I lay reading
Kafka.

2.
On some days
it's best to remain
crumpled in a ball
beneath the sheets
like a spider
feigning death.

3.
My old lover would
shriek at the sight of a spider. She left me
for a man with a kinder smile.

4.
Even in suburban households
wolf spiders crawl
like nightmares from the sinks.

5.
As the Buddha found
his eight-fold path
of awakening, a spider
descended the Bodhi tree
on a diamond string.

6.
The spider never sleeps
or so we think.

7.
I kept a spider
for a pet once—
his glass cage a monastic cell
and I the god
he despised.

8.
And on the eighth day
god awoke to discover
the spider, gone.

9.
O radiant skin cream angel I pray
a thousand baby spiders hatch
from your unwitting cheek.

10.
Before rain, the sky, swollen
with grey light: Somewhere
the spider must be feeding.

11.
When you wash a spider
down a drain, she's reborn,
an octopus.

12.
There is a kind of spider so large
it preys on birds. There are places
where everything is magnified.

13.
The earth at the end grew feverish.
Everything held its breath.
The spider unfolded its hidden wings
and fluttered toward the sun.

## Vanishing

My cat ran away the night
a great wind storm turned loose
the intrinsic wilderness waiting in everything.
I yelled into roiling torrents of air, *Hey there!*
*Frida cat! Frida calico! Frida kitty!*
for my companion of five years,
my confidante, my small
buffer against loneliness. The wind
maimed huge trees and the city awoke
to a confusion of leaves and limbs, a chaos
that destroyed summer overnight.
She never appeared again.

As the days slipped further
into the isolation darkness brings, my life
began to falter, as it regularly does
at this time, falling out of form, a vague
anxiety lurking in every shadowed
corner of every shadowed
room: the usual winter derangement.
But in confusion, I still searched
for sense, like how we draw designs
in the scattered stars or find shapes
in wind-blown clouds, in cigarette smoke, envision
patterns there, something nearly
self-aware. So I imagined her being
swept from the earth, lifted skyward
and moving toward this idea
of a magical intelligence.

Although her absence stayed with me
in my little apartment all winter long,
it waned each day, the ache
dissolving slowly inside the light
of the lengthening days, until
finally her name appeared
on memory's list of lost things
impractical to dwell on.

I must have learned to do this
in early childhood: to stop asking
bottomless questions, to abandon
the incomprehensible and surrender instead
to the kind-hearted lies my loved ones invented,
the *happily ever after* tales they told
to keep me quiet, to keep the wilderness
at bay—like my own inevitable
vanishing, the thought of being
less than one: such loneliness
impossible to imagine.

## After John Newlove

A miserly night sky, November
and Vancouver can promise only rain.

Grasping for a beginning: I've given everything
away, moved again, fled.

*What would you do John, make a list of fact?* Okay:
at a desk, at an unfamiliar night-blackened window, alone

at last. History gone, too—no personal past.
And I've seen the same girl working three nights

in a row on the street out there—her slow, elongated
stride, her pale face amidst the distant city lights—

like an actress before a constellation of eyes.
And this place—

where my little room, it's strange but true,
is painted pink, supposedly soothing

to the unsettled mind, some say—this place,
where a train's whistle claims nostalgia, near-

midnight and a suspicious lack of stars—
this place flickers in the night

like a radiant mind
inside a broken life.

And I wish John Newlove were here.
I'd ask him what the old days were like

sucking the blood from his abscessing tooth,
spitting out poems like divinely wrought curses.

*Was it the Age of Aquarius, John?*
*Or like me, did you crave some other city,*

*some other time, to ride*
*off any horizon, anywhere*

*but through this rain and the grey*
*eyes of the women you made so unkind?*

*Is this the same weather you let seep into your words,*
*your life? Did you hear poems inside the rain, or lies?*

Tonight, rain and loneliness have made me strange.
Or perhaps it's this pink room I'm in, like—

like a giant womb! Let's say it is
nineteen seventy-one. Unborn I am dreaming

of escape into the easy giving of the world's love.
Meanwhile, John Newlove wakes at the other end

of a long desire, rolls out of bed, rolls
a cigarette from Bible paper. Lighting the last page

of Genesis or maybe the first
of Revelations, he's suddenly tempted

by a girl outside his window, wants only
to give her words, redeem himself, repent

with savage eloquence, burn
a hole through the mist like a visionary...

Does any of this sound right, John?
I'm sure you lived here once.

Now everyone is gone.

*—Vancouver, 2001*

## *Das Ding an Sich* (The Thing in Itself)

Bits of sadly coloured nothing flash
between drops of rain: the greenish-grey
porous nature of reality. Frogs
in this weather can never quite
clear their throats, voices
stuck between high and low
intentions. For seven days and nights
I've remained afloat wanting nothing
else but to gently sink beneath the world
like an inverse cloud. How
much sorrow can this land take, this
ancient earth-lake? Of course, mud
is a meaningful medium, history-deep.
Here, like a vein of liquid silver or
the stem of a water orchid, a single
eyebrow quivers, the questioning
eyebrow of epistemology. Here,
where frogs linger, the rain
rains and eloquence
croaks.

# Room

Because the room knows
it can never go outside
I bring it things I think it will like:
peels of bark from the stylish arbutus,
the bones of tiny animals, their deaths
impossible as any to comprehend,
bits of broken bee hive and
pocketfuls of beach glass whose
hues have suffered beautifully
from many tides.

Because the room and I
have only lately become acquainted
we shyly waltz together
like red and blue ink inside
the clear water of silence
or stalk the slightest sound
like two wolves around a faltering doe.

Because the room still remembers
its previous guest leaving
so suddenly without warning or farewell,
it insists I change the locks, bar the windows,
give no one a second chance.

Because the room is lonely
I whisper a few words each morning
steady and soft like the incantation
of prayer, hoping the perfect phrase
will unlock the door the room keeps
deep within itself like a secret heart—
this door I'll walk through one day
and never return.

~2~

## Translations

We never say anything on the phone.
Instead the long distance of our breathing
seeps through the interstices of words where everything
unspoken speaks of what remains between us.
        I don't explain how, in the evenings,
I translate the sound of distant traffic into water
as it falls and purls into its deeper, placid self.
I say, *I'm fine*, but I guess you know what it's like
to live, besieged by rain, held captive by the sea, holed-up
in the shadow of mountains, and starved for more
than mere company.
        Do you remember the summer
we spent in bed, how after love our eyes would wander
out the north window, unreel above Burrard Inlet? I used to imagine
the mountains were prehistoric waves about to smash this town to bits
we might reconstruct one day into an image of whatever future
we desired. What you envisioned I never thought to ask.
        This was before the morning I awoke
to find I had somehow dreamt you into nothing
but the faint scent of your hair on the bedroom pillow,
before I came to recognize my own memories as nothing
but a succession of recurring themes akin to the orbit
of rosary beads worn dull by superstitious fingers.
But tonight,
        I wish I could I tell you something
more, that the person I once wanted you to be
still exists, miraculously, a voice that chatters and hums
as I write, a presence that sleeps beside me
even as I dream of the morning the rain came
to whisper with its innumerable silver tongues
of your departure.

## Lost in Transit

*to board a bus*
*is to step from this world*
*to another,*
*a small and private*
*transfiguration*

"Walking toward the bus station"— Alden Nowlan

***

The world is very small at the greyhound station.
Your destination is the size of a baggage tag,
your past, already fading like a bruise.

***

Lost in transit, everyone's a stranger
to themselves. First class means a window seat
where scenery affords the illusion
of solitude.

***

For a while the countryside flies by
like an otherworldliness and all you feel
is the transient's rush of belonging
only to this.

***

You cross the Fraser river
like a band of steel lined by trains
the colour of rust. Behind you now,
Vancouver's corrosion
vanishes.

***

Into the interior and dusk
where sage brush like balls of lightning
electrifies the hills.

***

At a rest stop you stretch
and entertain thoughts
of never arriving,
just wandering off and
disappearing from your life, telling no one
you've moved
to Kamloops.

***

Night. Small towns flash by
like meteor tails. Revelstoke, Golden…
Does anyone think of you passing
through darkness?

***

At dawn, a waterfall on the mountainside appears
white and soft as an angel's wing. Soon
you will descend into fields of grain.

***

Behind you, the Rockies
appear like a giant's hands
held over the eyes of the west.
Before you, the Prairies are
a vision quest, as your own eye,
starved, leans toward its private
universe.

***

You remember the Calgary depot
from another trip, the purgatory seats
with television sets that echo the news
from a world you only half belong to.
It's as if some phantom part of you
has been stuck here all these years,
waiting.

***

The miles unfold the hours but the hours
drag, as if unwilling to travel with you.

***

In this heat, thirty minutes
in Swift Current is enough.
The atmosphere is gelatinous.
The streets are mirrors of dust.
In Swift Current there is no current
swift enough.

***

Another late night diner stop augments
your weariness. Your waitress redefines fatigue.
Her complexion is chipped Formica
and the lines around her eyes like roadmaps
describe years of going
nowhere.

***

On the map Ontario is three centimetres across.
On the bus it takes forever plus one endless day.
You must be getting closer
to bureaucracy.

***

Your dreams are black
as a moonless ocean. The bus rolls on,
a wave with no shore in sight; your body,
a numbly coiled message in a bottle.

***

Heading into Sudbury
at three a.m. in hopeful delirium
you mistake the world's tallest smoke stack
for the CN Tower.

***

The last leg of the journey
is limping. You are a veteran
road-weary warrior, crazed
and unshaven. You know everything
about discomfort, what it means
to stagger
sitting down.

***

At the greyhound station the world
is still the same. Voices mingle, an endless
discordant strain in this place where no one belongs
unless we belong to each other's aches,
unless neither here nor there but
everywhere there are people there is this
common belief in movement,
and in arriving, one day,
at some final destination.

## What Do Writers Know?

—For J. Siddiqi

*I am not a painter, I am a poet.*
*Why? I think I would rather be*
*a painter, but I am not.*

"Why I am Not A Painter"—Frank O'Hara

I am two weeks in Montreal, the guest
of artists, crashing in their lofts, when suddenly
I envy painters, the physicality of their work:
canvasses stretched, trampoline-taut,
pigments ground from earth's own minerals and ores—
how the act of making becomes the *body's* grace,
the arm's gestures, the brush like a conductor's wand
directing a symphony of hues.

I envy them their well lit studios, their ability to move inside
a chamber of illuminated dreams. What do writers know
of such material wealth? Williams' decree, *No Ideas But in Things*
seems wasted on the poets, sickly step-children of the arts,
whose actions are more subdued: the dull hours of sitting
with crumpled brow, the prolonged bouts of staring
out the window, or at the screen as it slowly
fills with words, predictably, row upon row…

In my artlessness, I daydream painters
like Pollock and Riopelle, Monet and Van Gogh.
How I'd love to dribble eloquence from my tongue, splatter ink
with a mindless expressiveness indivisible from desire,
smudge or dab a line with a flourish of my wrist,
gesture a river into being or the green
sway of a cypress tree.

But lately it seems language demands
an inward fascination akin to neurosis
to bring it forth, a rare, self-obsessive
species of attention like a monk's
candle flame, its light falling exactly
inside the margins of a page.

Today it seems I must be content
to contain the world like the builder
of those bottled, miniature ships: every poem
a tiny still-life stuck behind a layer of polished glass—
where perhaps you can almost see, reflected here, my own
grimacing, ecstatic countenance, a kind of peripheral effect:
the cryptic wink of a self-portrait nearly
approaching the visual arts, and the closest
these words can come to the matter of human flesh.

## Montreal Backdrops

1.
Atop Mount Royal, tourists
have photos taken of themselves
against the cityscape, fail to imagine
the St. Lawrence river streaming
across their shoulders like a windblown scarf.

2.
Beneath the Autoroute, St. Henri
glows, each brick a different shade
of August twilight. Kids in this neighbourhood
sport the local regalia, mark the streets
with baseball hats, bandanas the colour
of traffic signs.

3.
On St. Denis, an (almost) blind
glass-throated mystic gargles
rhapsodic globes of phlegm, prophesies
oblivion. As a prank contrivance
of the squishy atmosphere, a game
of misdirection, a trickle of sweat sneaks
into his one good eye.

4.
At St. Catherine's sidewalk fair, vendors,
hell-bent on expounding the virtues of cheap
wrist watches, set the pace by which
pigeons bob their heads, move their feet
in convulsive, rhythmic jigs.

5.
Beside the creek of Parc Lafontaine people
read books, watch each other between the lines
while dogs, less demure, dive in, perform
the dog-paddle stroke, happy
and proud as idiots.

6.
In Old Montreal, new
industry booms where grain silos
like monumental tombs remain
ignored, vast, unexplored
echo chambers.

7.
At St. Joseph's Oratory
where Brother André's heart floats
inside a jar of murky light, to burn
a votive candle costs four dollars
and a prayer.

8.
Somewhere perhaps the future
ghost of Leonard Cohen moves
toward regret up an endless
flight of stairs.

9.
While you remain invisible,
a fixture of St. Laurent Boulevard.
Because you don't belong
you pretend to be a writer all summer,
sitting sequestered in the dark
café. If you could you'd construct
your own mythology, erect a language
equivalent to the city's bold façades.

10.
And now the fly, perched on your cappuccino cup,
rubs together its little arms.

# October, November, Toronto

*What does not change/is the will to change*

"Kingfishers"—Charles Olson

***

The oak in windy moonlight
outside the window, the resemblance
of an old love, dark hair
undulating, alive, her image
remembered, turning
to slow shadows
of leaves and bark again.

***

The old days:
the seditious heart and its luckless
skirmishes with affection; then
your sudden passage, your eastward quest:
a meteor blazing horizon to horizon,
Mercury, drunk and on the run.

***

Machines grumble. The ground
thunders. You wake thinking:
this could mean the end of the world
or just another Monday morning
of industry: what keeps everyone
carrying on.

***

The lack of landscape here: this city
is a map imposed upon a memory
of wilderness; your address, an abstraction
of numbers and old names that pretends
to contain your existence.

***

Morning, an encapsulation
of cold light. Swallows
circle the sun like crazy
moths around a fire at night.
Telephone wires confuse
the cityscape, a clash of horizons
and perspectives. Perhaps you are
half-asleep.

***

You shower and dress in clothes
made by strangers who exist
at the other end of the earth
without you in mind—fabric dyed
and sewn together without desire
in a place where no one lives alone.

***

Meanwhile, weather
has moved in. Suddenly
no birds, the air
a barren element. You are
walking now, thinking: why this
nervousness inside the chest
when fall arrives, the whispering
of windblown leaves that makes leaving
come to mind? How change evokes
the will's desire for change: why
the birds have gone and white clouds
materialize like dragons dragging
their tails across the sky.

***

Cold air shackles your wrists
as you dream of the easy home
you never had. Yes,
there is always the idea
a better place exists, but only
if you leave this one behind.

***

And always the sweet faces of friends
perpetually coming to your aid
to rob you of your necessary pain.

***

Today, you're the citizen
of a pale land: no monuments, just
chance preservations, moments
of still flesh: your body,
an institution; your mind, an archive
of misgivings.

***

Where can you go
from here? All your life
you've pretended to be
about to leave, but
the love she crafted, sharpened
to a single, unthinking
point, still pierces you.

***

Soon, tendrils of ice
will bar your windows, and the sun appear,
a white bead, a fragile fever.

***

And always the abstract desire
of prayer, poems: pages
of dry tears.

***

Machines grumble. The ground thunders. Who are you
to deny yourself this country, suddenly so huge
with undiscovered little towns?

## At the Greyhound Station

Feathered clouds spread above the Prairie, macrocosmic
of the osprey's glide: its detachment
from gravity and effortless style, patient
as a dust mote floating in God's blue
waiting room.

Grounded here
at the Greyhound station, a woman
flicks her cigarette at the curb, shuffles her feet,
kicks at stones like annoying
afterthoughts or fragments of remorse
stuck in the immovable July heat, and begins
to cry.

From where I stand—five provinces west
of the recent past, baggage in hand—from within
the context of my own misgivings, I imagine
she has tracked the winged creature of her innocence
across miles and years of thirst, that her journey
has been a series of advances and retreats, an incessant
readjustment of landscape, and always
the sad collapse of the exquisite vistas
her youth once led her to envision.

And I want our stories
to intertwine, fuse like two headlights
fixed on the road ahead, toward
some common destination.
I want to tell her that we're almost
there, far away from the city's buzz of nerves
like four million phones off the hook, and soon
to enter another world, the Kootenay's quiet enclave
of ponderosa pines and river-scented air.

Does she consider me at all, idly
wonder at my being here, her mind
sifting possibilities, searching for an excuse
to lessen the distance between us? But as I
take a step, she looks away, her eyes, sparrow-shy,
flitting past mine, a careless gesture, full
of implicit anonymity.

Cramped back into my seat
I am a solitary pilgrim again, the sky gone
faint behind the tint of my thin reflection;
while somewhere in the upper atmosphere
I envision a pair of wings slowly turning
like a compass needle above the small town
I've been so long looking for but can never find—
continually getting lost and falling in love
with a stranger's life.

~3~

## Hands

I.

October's first night,

like a stair I didn't
expect, a missed beat,

a discombobulating
plunge. Black windows

contain interiors bright
as teeth clenched

against the cold.
A certain mood grows

several pairs of hands,
strangles the air

like discordant jazz.
This is song

without melody,
the sick mind's habitual

involution like the zipping
and unzipping overture

of insomniac crickets, then
Coltrane, swinging alone

on the rusted hinge
of midnight, *A Love Supreme*

beneath an absence of stars.

II.

Sleep, a kind of love
I can keep. Hands like dead sparrows.

East of here is what you promised.
Fear, the moniker I didn't choose.

Infidelity, cheap rent. Mother
I'll see you soon.

Home is the place I never found.
Each window looked right through me.

How the bird with one leg flies
faster: Forget me like this.

Telling lies, I'm everything
I've always wanted to be: omnipotent, alone.

The myriad. What's that? Words of rain
we hear sometimes, without

listening.

III.

Goddamn Buddha on my desk,
uproarious. I've forgotten why.

Last blade of sun cuts through: meaning
everything in one faithless moment.

My mind, asleep, has always been here.
Five cigarettes a day. Steady job near the sea.

Three hard nights of idle solitude. Lines
abused by a soft and weakened hand.

The east: a mythology of distance.
The luminous space between words.

Glass of milk translucent on the kitchen table
says I've lost my recklessness.

Endlessly, one light burns.
Tonight, silence echoes

like the mirror image
of a mirror.

## Slip

I.

*I talk to a poet: he goes on, drunk:*
*I pray he's writing , don't dare ask.*

*Hang on, hang on: I'm listening,*
*I'm listening to myself.*

"Stilt Jack"—John Thompson

I have food I have cigarettes I have never enough
wine. There's John Thompson too. Ghazals. Drunk.

For all the worldly good it's done, for five months
I said little prayers at night.

Our intentions were always good. But now
let's talk about the weather: Let's say, *The sky's hand,*

*mailed in grey, menaces.* What's the point?
Just the forecast of tomorrow's dumb regret.

In this city, no one's home. I dive in, swim alone through
dark tunnel of telephone. Not one sweet voice.

Earlier you said:

I can feel my mind, creeping in:
Fear of madness. And the world. And now.

You are. Alone. The walls are speaking
gibberish. They say: to go on living like this

means suffering is a virtue
you love better than truth. The phone rings.

*Hello. Are you there?*
But I'm not home.

I'm with you.

II.

It is 7:28 a.m.

In my nightmare bullfrogs smile
like dolphins do. In my experience

what's repulsive eerily resembles
you. Myself, I am a common species

of brute, having originated nothing,
just complicated a few fundamental truths

throwing stones in the reflecting pool.
And now the moment of duplicity, furious

with tiny breaths, hungry
as a mosquito-dawn, is at hand.

It is 7:28 a.m.

But you are not listening
with the proper attention I had planned.

I envisioned you holding this poem to your ear
like a prehistoric seashell, like a phone

to the devil's heart, not running off to find yourself
without me, or, I fear, to tie one on,

to smear every wine glass in town
with the colour of your cheap lipstick.

It is 7:28 a.m.

O where are my waitresses with their tender words
and winks, their voices bright as the clink of silverware on plates?

There must have been a car crash or an earthquake or a falling
out of love. I mean, where are you anyway,

this *you* I speak of, this *you* I speak to, this *you*
I've yet to meet? Or were you with me

at the beginning? It was beautiful, the first city
I was deceived in. I fell upon my knees,

arms folded tightly around
the newborn creature panicking

inside my chest—that feeling.
I've gone looking for it ever since.

# Pillow Talk

For a time we waited for someone
beautiful to come along who would ask
the question which already contained,
within itself, the seed of an answer.

But what voice to choose, what words
to respond with? What thin music
would our soon-to-be exhausted throat
stretch across the years? Imagine

the trajectory of a cat's tail lithely
zigzagging through cords of rain, or a spider
trapped in a bathtub, its scuttling legs dancing
to the frenetic rhythms of its own tiny

done-for heart—

Here, like five wild dogs about to strike
a famished pose, five forms of self-pity
converge—here, at the point where tenderness
becomes a pain to be endured.

Or let's say this is where the five senses
sleep, deep inside the appraising dark
blue shadow cast by our guardian angel's
slowly beating wings.

How, ceaselessly invoked, our wine-
stained fingers tremble in the predatory moonlight.
Intertwined, they are the huddling idols
of a confession long overdue.

Now, one voice says, *Retire, sleep, give-in…*
while, beneath the bed, another voice
chatters its distress like a sack of teeth
being poured into an urn of polished bronze.

## Criticism

A crow cuts the dawn
to shreds, barks
its relentless invectives
down at what it must
think of as the pedestrian
world. Last night I unreeled
from gravity the delicate string
of my own ambition, floated up like a kite, like one
of the privileged elite, my arms and legs spread wide
to encompass the four corners of the earth,
my tongue bejewelled with opinions and conclusions
bright enough to vaporize heaven's tears—
suddenly awoke as less than half
of what, in my youth, I had expected
of my future self. What's worse
than being ridiculed, squawked at,
tricked into such knowledge?
            O evil-winged, saw-toothed
singer of misgivings, would you please
shut up for once. I was miles above
my prosaic flesh, happily dreaming
of death, or at least the end of self-
consciousness, my spirit ascending
a skeletal thread of light to the place
where everything precious is gained
without venture—until your strident abuses,
your feathers, black as the handles of knives
and the cutting blades of your throat.

## Interloper

I.

An urban cowboy lost in the wilderness,
your studies in style did not prepare you for this—

Breezes whisper
gibberish through the unidentifiable
undergrowth, a vocabulary
of tiny devils clattering
the pointy sticks of their tongues.

What follows is the silence
of a wilderness that refers
to nothing but itself.
Only the mouths of stones
hold breath.

Pines no longer
pines distort into green
ladders, limbs like rungs
enticing vertigo, depth's
inverse, a way out—

Somewhere the city hums the tune
of a grand machine functioning without
you in mind. Your home,
a vacant room rented and invented
from arbitrary space, awaits

no one. How long
before your friends
grow small and imperious
as the faces on coins
and your body belongs solely

to survival? How long
until you descend the ravine
to the dry river bed, where
between boulders, gravid
with timelessness, dragonflies

unstitch the air with wings, opal
as the opening eyes of dusk, and you
are pulled toward the cold,
and night plucks from you one by one
your multifold disguises—

II.

An urban cowboy lost in the wilderness,
your studies in style did not prepare you for this—

Birds in the trees like exotic women giggle
at your spurs made out of tin, your hat
like a ten-gallon satellite dish tuned
to Hollywood's version of manhood
and your feet as they trip over tree roots
the same way your tongue stumbles
over the names of places you've never been.

Drifter, stranger to these parts
but without mystique, your life is a movie
that no one would ever pay to see. Only the eyes
of animals are upon you, amused
by the huge shadow you tow behind
like some soundless, sullen companion.

It's not the sunset you ride into finally,
but the halogen glare of your old home town,
where image is everything and nothing
seems real anymore, where suburbs sprawl
like graveyards beyond the periphery
of your awareness and you dream
tombstones the size of skyscrapers.

Perhaps now you'll become a citizen, one
of many souls with a role to bear within a maze of glass-
sculpted architecture, lost inside a soundscape
of staccato jazz footsteps and the city's
low hum, each street like a cubist's idea
of a river you must cross—your life,
an unnatural disaster waiting for its chance,
like winning the lottery or love
at first glance.

Perhaps now you'll choose whiskey
in lieu of wilderness, oblivion
over freedom, the tavern's life of telling lies
about your youth, of growing old
before your time. Night after night
you'll squint into the distance like a legend, kiss
the stale air with a smile, trying to recall
what it was you never found.

## Enemy Number One

*The problem with poetry is poets*

"You"—Ron Silliman

He has not been properly concerned
with poetry; she tells him, she
who dislikes the word *academic*,
that language is a socio-political construct
whose purpose is to codify, that is
perpetuate positions of power, that no word
is without sex, class or race affiliations, and

poetry, well poetry these days
is only language that's been obsessed over,
tricked into revealing itself—at its best
a progressive act, a way to disrupt
hierarchy, corrupt hegemony and evade
the cuts and blows and perfumes
of subjectively entrenched lyricism. And

when she tells him this he understands
it is not poetry he has lately been so
concerned with, but more a love
of telling beautiful lies, the sexual pliancy
of language: imperfect words
he shapes like tools and weapons
to perpetuate his life.

# Exposé

*1. Witness*

Eyes mechanically
flick open, shut, open,
strobe the world into a slide show
vision of the world
unfolding.

*2. Buzz*

No doubt the ears
attuned and shaped
like Venus Fly Traps
were designed to digest
living morsels of air.

*3. Perfume*

Nostalgia's dank portal:
who knows how the nose
remembers, evokes the subtle
textures of long-ago
emotions, but not events?

*4. Mute*

Anxious lips pop, breath
catches, hooks and flits around
the bewildered tongue
like a windblown scarf
caught in a leafless tree.

*5. Suffer*

To be precise the skin
does not crawl, it leaps
distractedly from point
to point, piecemeal going
everywhere.

## Happiness Will Come

Yesterday you claimed: happiness will come
stumbling in at last, fists full of crazy
daffodils and stalks of pampas grass,
so long as the broken wanderer returns
penniless as a newborn—

Forgetfully you promised: the sky will grow
tendrils of light visible as curlicues at the bottom of water,
like a dream of hieroglyphs or a soft chandelier,
so long as an old friend arrives unannounced
and with him the surprise of newly fallen snow—

But I predict: sadness will curl up
like a comma, like a soldier hunkered down
inside the cold womb of his bunker,
so long as you remain here with your sexless conversation
and the wonderful ornaments of your body concealed.

## Before

Stillness
was everything's innate delight—
the laughing Buddha atop the bookshelf,
its crystallized appreciation of the undisturbed
dust motes suspended in time like stars—
before you waltzed in,
the materials of your mind spinning
in orbits all around you.

Although you can't recall,
it was exactly like before
you were born, when you looked down
from your existence before time and saw
all movement poised on the perpetual
brink of itself, then wondered
*how* or *why* or some such thing
and sent every electron and galaxy wheeling...

## Body of Evidence

Somewhere between PEI
and Kathmandu, I choose
to live inside a culture
that lives outside of culture.
And so I choose to dwell
in formlessness. Still,
language exists, a tiny
convoluted animal, a snail
curled up inside the ear
like a smaller brain.
This is where
every part of the body
misbehaves. Each knuckle
of my fist stares up
like an angry eye.
My lips let slip the tune
of falling bombs.
As such, the physical
makes invisible sense,
makes indisputable fact
out of thin air. For instance,
how you exist, miraculously
pulling this string of words along
until, like the slipknot of a dream,
my testimony reveals itself
as just another trick
I have invented
to deceive you with.

## As It Is in Heaven?

Opening the Gideon's Bible
in the private loneliness
of my hotel room, I walk
this carpet stripy as a television screen
with no horizontal control, pace
in slippers made from clouds
I pulled down myself
from the shelf of civilization's
last Dollar Store.
          Distractedly, I scratch,
this dry, ethereal mountain town
air transforming my skin into
an aura of dust, bright as flour
in a bakery owned and run
by smiling cherubs and light-
footed angels.
          Perhaps it was
in this very world and not
so long ago when The Ultimate
Solipsist said, and I quote:
*I am that I am*, which, to me,
implies an hermetically sealed
causal loop, a perfectly self-
contained universe.
          Is it exactly like the way
I now sit, hunched here within this
ergonomically designed chair, my spine
quarrelling with concordance?
No,
          so far from the city's
snug mythology and lost to my own
history of jaded disbelief, it is more
like how I mistook, mysteriously, just now,
my face in the page's white mirror
for another's, for a stranger's,
for the unknown face
of my father—

# Escaping the Foreground

I.

Morning's light on the waves
is a flickering of the sea's
private joy, deep delight
breaking the surface
in haphazard flashes
of diamond-white—
or just a chimera, a peripheral
distraction, another of the eye's
Machiavellian attempts
at beauty?

This is how you steal
into the morning, cautiously
stepping over barnacles—
their craggy shells like eyes
clenched shut against
the orgiastic seaweeds, limp-lying,
the colour of old blood.

What are you doing here?
At this hour, the moon
like an ill-mannered party guest
is still hanging around,
a translucent film of its former self,
ashamed, reluctant, perhaps
paralysed by daylight—

while the wind, as always, is determined
to be gone, knowing nothing,
moving through the shoreline trees,
animal-soft, alive

in the dying sound of leaves.

II.

The freedom the eye knows, resting
in the distance beyond detail, sky and ocean
merged in a seamless union where not even the idea
of you, or anyone else, exists.

Staring out across the silent Pacific
into this broadening bell of clear space, you've come
to forget the way the most difficult forms
inhabit the smallest spaces: *love*

written at the bottom of a letter,
the city lights you've fled, sealed up neatly
like a flame inside a pocket lighter,
your own perplexing ache...

Here, the eye floats away
like a stringless kite above the sea—
this one part of you, at least, escaping
the foreground while another still desires

clarification, stubbornly remains fixed
at the edge of the world, believing
there is always more to understand: your mind,
a tiny crack in the fine crystal of oblivion

as the eye withdraws again, sudden as a breeze
over the water's surface, to this ancient
sandstone beach tormented by storms and tides,
licked into sinuous shapes, contorted figures

with faces, grimacing and ecstatic—
this fantastic community of suffering,
to which, even here,
you belong.

~4~

# Nowhere But Here (Vancouver)

I.

We are
denizens of a dim land,
children with grey
rainbows. Sullen eyes
and mouths pattern the air
like wings afloat, shadow-
thin above bodies
of polluted water. Only
the stranger of ourselves
reflected in
silvered glass, in
the chromatic anarchy
of gasoline spills, in
the shards of broken
promises, can see beyond
our feigned insouciance, peer
deep into the night's disgrace, where
white feathers soaked in blood
litter the alleyways, the gutters
of paradise, where
climbing the stairs the rain makes in
gusts of wind, we know
we'll never arrive, never
even leave the ground.

II.

Red tongue at night, the flame's
yawn wavers, sexualizes
the dying of the light. Streets shed
their lithe ghosts. Armies of mist
advance upon the Milky Way, vengeful
corpses seeking the terminal
kingdom. If we say all hope
is meaningless it's still
a moot point, futile
as the moon's halo rigged
like a slipknot noose. God, free us
from belief in Absolutes. Tonight
an unloved innocent wearing nothing
but a pair of fleecy slippers
and a grin will slip beyond the stars
and drown out of downright pity
for himself. Something's wrong, obviously,
with the therapists in this town and maybe
the meteorologists too. Like the rain,
the inarticulate and helpless confess
in a panoply of whispers that reflect
the liquid surface of our fears. Listen:
some are wicked or crazy, while a few
have tasted the lawless truth.

III.

Sure fortune smiles
and laughs too, an exploding
cornucopia, cacophonous as a fist-sized
stone through a store window.
These streets are rampant
with hopeful souls: dime-a-dozen
losers scratching scratch-and-wins,
unkempt pie-in-the-sky types, my friends
and neighbours, the mythic
Lumpenproletariat! But do we truly
believe hope is on its way? Yesterday

we resisted the Corporate Zeitgeist,
nailed our disillusionment to the local
laundromat notice board.
Today we gather on the left side
of town, listen to the ghost
of Karl Marx (disguised as a Turkish hot dog
vendor) promise the revolution
will be bloodless and sweet
as ketchup, and the price of freedom
will include tax. Meanwhile,
down the block, behind
the Buddhist monastery, the re-incarnation
of Elvis as the A&W Root Beer Bear
is either an honest greasy fact or
just another progressive City Councillor
drunkenly waving his fists in the air
like maracas on fire. Obviously
his message is hallucinatory,
duplicitous, slippery,
blood-hot. But we the people
could care less about his immoral plots.
The pedestrian light flashes,
provokes universal automatism
and good cheer. At once I become
like you, like everyone here: merciless,
tunelessly whistling, stepping
like the hand of a clock
into an endlessly near
future.

IV.

Strange,
how we are here,
either sorrowfully
alone or together
in discord, all of us
in this city, this institution,
this barroom of mutable darkness
where our shadows blur like the fingers
of an insomniac pianist improvising
cacophonic jazz...which is why
the other musicians will soon
abandon the song, usurped by notes like
shattering nerves of glass.
            It is inescapable, the way
this ends: The bass player
must waltz his instrument gently
to the floorboards, lay it on its side as if
it were an invalid lover.
The drummer must check his watch,
decide it's time to switch from beer
to scotch and conclude that his faith
in the existence of an audience
has failed again—unless he considers
the sullen-eyed one, the one who arrives
too late, who sits alone, feeling betrayed
by his own ambition and tenderly stroking the wound
his prematurely severed youth
left him with.
Listen,
            sorrow's ways are myriad
and unidentifiable as footsteps
creaking the sanatorium floorboards
in the common dark. Now night skulks into
the room and with it, the smell of impending rain.
Now we could be listening to a phone ring
in a dream, the way, lost inside the intricacies
of an unchecked desire, the pianist describes
the city he was ruined in.

## Idiolect

Thirty years ago today, I was born
in Montreal with a name
I couldn't comprehend. On that day
I imagine the Saint Laurence river
chugged along, the colour of an old wartime nickel,
the colour of a nickeless nickel let's say,
a shiny kind of poverty. Well, who knows
how to describe the daedal surfaces
of history, memory's intangible misgivings. Foolishly
I remember in order to exceed the confines of my life,
speak to flood the margins of intelligence
like a kid wanting more
colouring outside the lines.

As a kid I didn't speak to anyone,
hid and watched from beneath the table
for the first two weeks of school. Thirty
years later, I'm still here, wondering,
where did Ursula Snyder go, in her
pigtail bows and overalls? The girl
everyone called *Snyder Wieners*
whom I secretly adored
and for whom I developed a silent language,
a kind of emotional semaphore, a failing
at love—I mean to say *flailing* like
a comedian descending through time
and space without a parachute who
flaps his arms. *Tempus fugit.*

Like this I've fallen through
the humourless centre, endured
long hours of trudging mediocrity,
the melting clocks, the solar flares, the liquid art
of compromise. I've traveled far beyond success
to many disappointments, to the periphery
of loserville, yes, here, to the shores
of linguistic ruin, preferring this to other
allegedly transcendental thrills like
political speech writing or
hang-gliding naked or
the two-cent whiz-bang apocalypse of sex
without love. *Ephemeron*
*ad infinitum.* It's true,

I once wanted that
one thing more or that one thing less, i.e.
*happiness.* Now, sitting here, sifting through
the detritus of the years, the fingers
of my tongue slipping around the myriad
names and places I once knew or imagined
I knew at one time—now, I want only to resist
the fleeting textures of experience,
burnish these lies of memory, I mean *lines*
against my knucklebone.

# In the Changing History

In the Early Romantic painting,
light strums the silent lyre
of the water's surface.

Here, to be in love with solitude
is the ideal.
Suddenly, I want nothing

of skyscraping aestheticism
or its cagey, mercurial
practitioners.

In the city,
as in the changing history
of each moment,

success breathes life
into innumerable failures.
Here, we are citizens of the earth

in exile, we
who murder our erotic bodies
with redundant blows,

our moans
recalling the so-called
shocking events

from yesterday's headlines.
Somnolent and sluggish
each letter fumes, rolls

over and over
in the slow-motion style
of a flaming car wreck.

Its light consumes the world.

## At the Park

Stripped of self-
pity I am
genuinely sorry
for myself.
            Yes,
knowing there's nothing
to complain about
is a good reason
to feel lost.
            In public,
where is it
publicly
acceptable
to be alone?
            At the park,
I don't begrudge
the weeping willow
its green fountain
of tears,
            only
how lovers find
comfort there, inhabit
the twilight beneath
its canopy.
            Moreover,
this matter of beauty I can't explain:
if lust is desire without artifice,
then what to assume
about the peacock's stroll?
            Love,
says the cynic,
is based on a mutual
emptiness. I submit:
this resolves nothing
            relative

to my new friend's affection:
the little unwitting
freak suddenly
beside me on my bench:
            an albino squirrel,
happily munching
a cigarette butt—
eyes the colour
of roses.

## Not Quite Winter

November. The sky is missing:
a stolen monument, a breach. Still,
a few starlings litter the horizon: distant
flickerings, variegated shades of ash. Meanwhile,

a cross-hatched scrim or
a tangled mess of wind-
nodding tree limbs complicates
optimism. Knowing

the season, the attic chatters, a home
to scurrilous squirrels, mischief's minions,
inclined to strident and obnoxious idioms.
Knowing as little or

as much, I mutter myself, pace the unvarnished
floorboards in circular logic, consider what
and what's not meant to be.
Awake or asleep

I am a slave to my circadian rhythms,
just as the sun like a golden coin or
a nameless smear ascends or descends on time.
Now is the season, the hour

well into the festival of what is not eternal,
and always the theme of poetry
as involution and/or the winter blahs.
Now comes the too sudden

darkness and the skinless moon:
a lidless eye or maybe it's just God's
bare light bulb dangling from oblivion.
Yes, in such light

I'll compose my book
of winter, let pages flutter
to the floor, accumulate one by one
like flakes of snow, senseless, cold,

full of essence.

## New Year's from Space

Innumerable
voices collide, spark
pure as reason
inside a vacuum.
          Sure,
the future smiles
and winks
like a glass diamond
in the snow.
          Remember
how the empty
summons
of a train's whistle
once turned the night
          around
the usual vagrants
vacillating beneath
the childish moon, the dead
gnarled oak? Still, there is
          nowhere
to go but slowly
nowhere, creeping toward
ignorance of what
the future holds, and what
          if
existence is
parenthetical
and time
never ends?
          Suddenly
it's January first, two-thousand and…
like a stillborn wind
or a ghost at my throat,
or the shivering fingers of stars.

## Our Friend

There are traces of his absence
everywhere: abandoned cigarettes
burn in ashtrays just after last call,
pairs of shoes appear dangling
like inedible fruit from power lines,
broken umbrellas prop up
the corners of waiting rooms,
pennies glow on the twilit sidewalk
bright as fool's gold.
        Irrefutably, he exists, although the world
has placed him in a drawer labelled
*miscellaneous*. He's a word in a language
no one speaks anymore, a rosary bead
broken from its orbit, a prayer
fallen back to earth, a stone
down a wishing well.
        It's as if, metaphysically speaking,
his heart's been beat to airy
nothingness. We've lost his name
somewhere within the countless cells
of our own flesh, impossible
to negotiate as the distance
between stars.
        Perhaps we picture him
characteristically
somewhere else, slumped
in an alleyway, immersed
in Chinese wine, or kneeling
in a church basement sweating
coins for his sins, or seated
on a bus, riding forever
to the edge of town. We might think
of Prince Charming
in exile or a socially inept
introvert. But remember, the solitary
figure stumbling through the night
inside our mind is only someone
we've invented to legitimize our quiet
un-protesting life.

Perhaps we imagine
on a dark wet corner of the city, cloaked
in anonymity, lost like the moon behind
a windblown cloud, our friend
breeds animal-lusts, insect-appetites,
inhuman desires inside the grey swamp
of his mind. Of course he doesn't
share our vision of him
as a one-legged crow hopping along,
pain-stabbed, each feather
a bristling black, misanthropic
flame. He knows his misfortune
has nothing to do with this shifting
darkness, knows shadows
are more than the absence of light.
Or do we perceive his elusiveness
as an indication of some turbid
inner life, DNA strands undulating
like wind toys in the molecular breeze of his cells?
Do we diagnose our friend as the victim
of some neurological flaw
and confine him for life inside
the primitive antechambers of the brain?
Do we suspect our friend
of overindulgence, force him to walk
an invisible line with closed eyes?
But this is the guesswork of bad science.
This is religion gone wrong.
And if, one day, our faith disintegrates,
if our words grasp for meaning and
miss, if love turns and pins us down
in an intimacy of punishment
and slugs our skull again and again
into an uncharted starry realm,
will we declare a state of war
against some celestial hegemony,
start aiming rockets at the moon?
But this is Job without piety. This is fear.
This is seeing our friend's absence
as only absence. Instead let's see it
as proof that he exists

everywhere, moves
in all directions, murmurs
sadly on the periphery
of our willingness to listen,
stands at the vanishing point of time—
his inscrutable identity, a secret
we'll soon need to discover
in order to survive.

## For You

*Twice or thrice had I loved thee,*
*Before I knew thy face or name*

"Air and Angels"— John Donne

If, unwittingly, I have brushed
you aside, bruised or broken you
in my riotous passage,
I apologize.

Know that I have felt the same
sting of love discovered then lost
in the time it takes a thought to pass,
that instant of imagined recognition,
epiphany invented from an accidental
glance or touch.

Consider last night, how I thought
you laughed with me from across the room
at the absurd beauty of things beyond
our powers to charm, how this morning
faint birdsong took me from a dream and I
awoke alone again.

For you then—
who have perhaps also discovered me
capable of neither sweetness nor tangibility—
these words.

## When Will Your Real Life Begin?

. . . your other life, the one
you've been holding out for?
Will it be anything like what you left behind
or more like what someone long ago
promised the future held?
(though who this was you can't remember).
Lately the city, like a kind of presence
you can't account for keeps creeping
in beneath the door at night. Nebulous
shadow dispossessed of matter
it huddles in the corner, listening
to the silence and how you answer it
with the same question again
and again: When will it begin,
the first morning of your real life, when
will it begin?

## The *Mad Rush* of Philip Glass

You hear everything at once buzz of electricity voices of rain in the trees voices from Robson Street swish of tires on wet pavement dog's mechanical barking barking someone taking the stairs on the fly someone perhaps surmounting a series of obstacles with resounding leaps and bounds while you imagine you hear far beneath it all the low hum of the city like a pipe organ underground a sustained note unwavering and still as the eye of a storm all things revolving around and around like the *Mad Rush* of Philip Glass a gyroscope in love with the sound of its own whirring an airtight philosophy tossed from a bridge pages spinning forever in space forever describing the endless beginning of a circular argument like your own self-perpetuating appetite your desire for experience the carnival-ride thrill of daring the periphery the ecstatic eye's panoramic view everyone's face an indissoluble blur the riot in your ears the whiz of blood in a centrifuge yet still you imagine a place without such velocity without the hullabaloo of human endeavours to pursue or avoid a place without clocks or wheels or words somewhere miles or centuries from here thinking what pleasure stillness would be to possess the white centre yet what terror to hear the lone beat of your heart endlessly endlessly...

# The Sun

When the sun is a presence in the room, its warmth on your stiff neck a lingering erotic peace: the same feeling a lover once left you with, a gorgeousness you mistook for love; when a super-heated ball of gas millions of miles removed away in space comes on to you in the middle of the afternoon—expect only to surrender to the day as it surrounds your immobility; as silence like gentle music ripples out in every direction; as motes of dust meander inside the leaves of the prayer plant—leaves like hands splayed open, worshipping this midday light—and as each moment sleeps in time, a lazy transcendence like the easy way insight once came to you after a few too many drinks: how the world seemed suddenly all-significant and all-resembling, an infinity of metaphor...how today the sun seeks only minuscule things, prefers the tiny gold hairs of your arm.

# May Jazz

—For Marc Church

Soft air
delicately cut
and sutured, jazz
stitched. You see this
everywhere: Daffodils
in meandering rows
bow their heads,
nod their brassy halos
to the rhythm of raindrops,
slow-dance to the cadence
of drizzle, to the last notes
of spring. And you hear this
in the wind-rippled grass, the jazz
cymbal's final, prolonged hiss—
and your grief suddenly
hushed within this
liquid sibilance.

## Singing in the Wings

A good day, any day above ground
where what's lost stays lost and what's found remains
as long as it takes for breath to swing around
the fulcrum of a hummingbird's throat.

Flight, a kind of a singing in the wings,
peripheral sotto voices, or buried
tongues intermingling like tree roots,
curling erotically like toes?

To proselytize. To galvanize. Think of Coltrane,
nailing it to the ground, stepping off
the bus at dusk in a Byzantium forged
from medallions of coppery light.

Listen: the bumble bee is no tenor.
His single, prolonged, fuzz-cello note, suspended
in the air like a cordless vibration, is all he knows
of rapture, of transport.

## Anna's Kitchen

—After Paul Durcan's "Teresa's Bar"

We would sit all day in Anna's kitchen,
in the ramshackle expanse of her care,
quaffing bottomless cups of coffee,
consuming the waffles and eggs she cooked
while the cat with its unpolished manners
trotted across the cluttered table,
to and from the open window, happy no doubt
to be in the thick of things, cutting through
the cigarette smoke and the talk
of the winter just passed,
of the crazy old days when the world
was forever coming to an end—
yet the soft surprise of having made it here
and the things we were all now set on doing
in this strange bright breaking
of a new millennium.
And the light in Anna's kitchen would thicken
in the lazy afternoons, its radiance bundle
more tightly around the passing time,
slowing it down 'till it came to rest
in Anna's eyes:
Anna's eyes
like brown birds against the sun,
Anna, healer of love-lives gone awry
and eager confessor to her own past
or more recent brushes with affection,
Anna, matriarch of the mornings
and afternoons, the image of serenity
and complete abandon,
and the splendour of all of this:
such important days of doing nothing
more than basking in her devotion,
the easy bestowing of her love,
the heaven of her kitchen,
and we, like children again, anticipating
the eternal days
of summer
to come.

# Of Two Minds

Above the flood of noon-hour traffic
and swarming sidewalks we look
from your second-storey apartment
to the west: A thick shield of clouds
divides the sky. Then the sun
breaks free: a mellifluous golden crash,
tambourines of light through the window
as your black cat hides
beneath the bed.

Of two minds,
I stop, mid-phrase, feel
the tangled rope of my throat
tighten, knot to knuckles
of a cocked fist. This could be
the moment when justification falters,
cruelty begins and the hurtful,
irrevocable words, true or not,
split the air.

Outside, you and I,
on the fire escape, we climb
towards the rooftop. Six storeys
closer to God, you say. We lie
on our backs, the soft tar
like flesh to touch, like the olives
we have brought to eat. I imagine
your skin, the taste of salt
and darkness on my tongue.
We spit into the air the tiny hard hearts,
visualise the sheer drop.

Once again, the sun is swallowed.
Clouds like dark authoritative hands
descend, and with them a sudden breeze
which rearranges the molecules of the atmosphere
into rain and an uncertainty my mind
translates into a new kind of fear,
as I think:

*There is no place in the world*
*for miracles, just this weight*
*of longing*—then what
it would be like,
without reason,
to jump—

## Variation on a Theme

—For Teresa

It's the timing that's important,
the incessant, eternal music of things
like waiting for the red wine to hit
before you smoke your last cigarette
mingling the two together
for that small but perfect ache
on an evening such as this:

Another glass to prolong the moment
since you can't sleep anyway; only
the cat is lost in its important slumber.
But listen: on the radio, Glenn Gould
hums off-key behind his piano—
the way you too sing
these crude little songs
to keep the whole universe
company.